Vendor Market LogBook

Table of Content

1 Subscription/Renewal/Membership

2 Overhead Expenses

4 Other Costs to Prepare for Sales

12 Inventory Turnover

16 Start-Up Basic Items

17 Vehicle Maintenance

18 Gas/Fuel Expenses

22 Mileage Log

32 Farmers Markets Vendor Fees

37 Events, Shows & Festivals Vendor Fees

41 Cash Pymt Activity Overview

43 Paypal/Square Pymt Activity Overview

49 Meals/Food Expenses

56 Blanks Pages

SUBSCRIPTION/RENEWAL/MEMBERSHIP

Pay on a Yearly Plan	Fee/Cost ($)
Business Insurance	
Business License	
Domain Name	
Web Hosting Plan	
Shipstation	
Amazon	
Costco	

OVERHEAD EXPENSES
Monthly Overview

	Rent	Gas/Electric	Water	Phone
JAN				
FEB				
MAR				
APR				
MAY				
JUN				
JUL				
AUG				
SEP				
OCT				
NOV				
DEC				

JAN				
FEB				
MAR				
APR				
MAY				
JUN				
JUL				
AUG				
SEP				
OCT				
NOV				
DEC				

OVERHEAD EXPENSES
Monthly Overview

	Rent	Gas/Electric	Water	Phone
JAN				
FEB				
MAR				
APR				
MAY				
JUN				
JUL				
AUG				
SEP				
OCT				
NOV				
DEC				

JAN				
FEB				
MAR				
APR				
MAY				
JUN				
JUL				
AUG				
SEP				
OCT				
NOV				
DEC				

OTHER COSTS TO PREPARE FOR SALES

Costs you incur to prepare your products for sale

Items/Products	Cost ($)
PaperMart Glassine bags, shrinks bands, treat bags, gift bags, lip balm tubes, beeswax, push-up deodorant tubes, round steel tin cans, labels	$388.92

OTHER COSTS TO PREPARE FOR SALES

Costs you incur to prepare your products for sale

Items/Products	Cost ($)

OTHER COSTS TO PREPARE FOR SALES

Costs you incur to prepare your products for sale

Items/Products	Cost ($)

OTHER COSTS TO PREPARE FOR SALES

Costs you incur to prepare your products for sale

Items/Products	Cost ($)

OTHER COSTS TO PREPARE FOR SALES

Costs you incur to prepare your products for sale

Items/Products	Cost ($)

OTHER COSTS TO PREPARE FOR SALES

Costs you incur to prepare your products for sale

Items/Products	Cost ($)

OTHER COSTS TO PREPARE FOR SALES

Costs you incur to prepare your products for sale

Items/Products	Cost ($)

OTHER COSTS TO PREPARE FOR SALES

Costs you incur to prepare your products for sale

Items/Products	Cost ($)

INVENTORY TURNOVER

SKU	Products	In Sock	Sold	Make/ Purchase
SLEM	Soap_Lemon	94	31	48
DMAX	Deodorant_MAX	8	7	15

INVENTORY TURNOVER

SKU	Products	In Sock	Sold	Make/ Purchase

INVENTORY TURNOVER

SKU	Products	In Sock	Sold	Make/ Purchase

INVENTORY TURNOVER

SKU	Products	In Sock	Sold	Make/ Purchase

START-UP BASIC ITEMS

Farmers Markets/Events/Shows/Festivals

Just a few things....	Cost ($)
10X10Ft Tent(s)/Canopy	
8 Ft Table(s)	
Tableclothe(s)	
Display boxes	
Chair(s)	
Business cards	
Bags/gift bags	
Cash box	
POS device (Square/Paypal)	
Portable power station	
4 Tent weights filled with rocks/sand	
3 - 4 Tarps & Clasps	
2 Floodlight(s)	
Handtruck/Folding Wagon Cart	
2 Calendars (1 Large-print & 1 Pocket-size)	
2 Expandable File Folder	

VEHICLE MAINTENANCE

For Optimum Vehicle Performance

Service/Repairs	Cost ($)
Battery	
Brake fluid	
Brakes	
Car wash/vacuum	
Coolant/Anti-freeze	
Head/rear lights	
Jumper cables	
Motor oil	
New Service vehicle	
Smog check/Car Registration	
Tires	
Transmission fluid	
Tune-ups	
Windshield wipers	

GAS/FUEL EXPENSES

Date	Odometer	km/ Miles	Liter/ Gallons	Cost ($)
Oct 12, 2016	150944	261	9.64	$27.51
Oct 28, 2016	151213	269	9.6	$31.40

GAS/FUEL EXPENSES

Date	Odometer	km/ Miles	Liter/ Gallons	Cost ($)

GAS/FUEL EXPENSES

Date	Odometer	km/ Miles	Liter/ Gallons	Cost ($)

GAS/FUEL EXPENSES

Date	Odometer	km/ Miles	Liter/ Gallons	Cost ($)

MILEAGE LOG

Date	Destination	Start Odometer	End Odometer
Oct 27, 2017	Bernardo Winery FM	150944	150971
	Ericson Elem School	150971	150981
	Home	150981	151007

MILEAGE LOG

Date	Destination	Start Odometer	End Odometer

MILEAGE LOG

Date	Destination	Start Odometer	End Odometer

MILEAGE LOG

Date	Destination	Start Odometer	End Odometer

MILEAGE LOG

Date	Destination	Start Odometer	End Odometer

MILEAGE LOG

Date	Destination	Start Odometer	End Odometer

MILEAGE LOG

Date	Destination	Start Odometer	End Odometer

MILEAGE LOG

Date	Destination	Start Odometer	End Odometer

MILEAGE LOG

Date	Destination	Start Odometer	End Odometer

MILEAGE LOG

Date	Destination	Start Odometer	End Odometer

FARMERS MARKETS VENDOR FEES
Space Fee & Direct Mkgt Fee

FM Vendors Reciepts	Fee	Gross Sales	Parking
Ocean Beach Farmers Mkt	$42	$470.25	$5.00

FARMERS MARKETS VENDOR FEES

Space Fee & Direct Mkgt Fee

FM Vendors Reciepts	Fee	Gross Sales	Parking

FARMERS MARKETS VENDOR FEES
Space Fee & Direct Mkgt Fee

FM Vendors Reciepts	Fee	Gross Sales	Parking

FARMERS MARKETS VENDOR FEES
Space Fee & Direct Mkgt Fee

FM Vendors Reciepts	Fee	Gross Sales	Parking

FARMERS MARKETS VENDOR FEES
Space Fee & Direct Mkgt Fee

FM Vendors Reciepts	Fee	Gross Sales	Parking

EVENTS, SHOWS & FESTIVALS VENDOR FEES
Vendor, Booth & Advertising Fees

Events/Shows	Fee	Gross Sales
El Cajon Victorian Country Christmas	$75	$1099.60

EVENTS, SHOWS & FESTIVALS VENDOR FEES

Vendor, Booth & Advertising Fees

Events/Shows	Fee	Gross Sales

EVENTS, SHOWS & FESTIVALS VENDOR FEES

Vendor, Booth & Advertising Fees

Events/Shows	Fee	Gross Sales

EVENTS, SHOWS & FESTIVALS VENDOR FEES
Vendor, Booth & Advertising Fees

Events/Shows	Fee	Gross Sales

CASH PYMT ACTIVITY OVERVIEW
Daily Gross Sales

Date	Events/Shows	Cash	Other
6/17	Chula Vista Lemon Fest	$238.43	

CASH PYMT ACTIVITY OVERVIEW
Daily Gross Sales

Date	Events/Shows	Cash	Other

PAYPAL/SQUARE PYMT ACTIVITY OVERVIEW
Daily Gross Sales

Date	Events/Shows	Square	Paypal
6/14	St. Rita Church Bazaar	$998.70	

PAYPAL/SQUARE PYMT ACTIVITY OVERVIEW
Daily Gross Sales

Date	Events/Shows	Square	Paypal

PAYPAL/SQUARE PYMT ACTIVITY OVERVIEW
Daily Gross Sales

Date	Events/Shows	Square	Paypal

PAYPAL/SQUARE PYMT ACTIVITY OVERVIEW
Daily Gross Sales

Date	Events/Shows	Square	Paypal

PAYPAL/SQUARE PYMT ACTIVITY OVERVIEW
Daily Gross Sales

Date	Events/Shows	Square	Paypal

PAYPAL/SQUARE PYMT ACTIVITY OVERVIEW
Daily Gross Sales

Date	Events/Shows	Square	Paypal

MEALS/FOOD EXPENSES

Breakfast	Lunch	Dinner
McDonald's Sandwich, coffee hash browns 10/28 $6.89	Greek platter cookies candied apple $13	Street Tacos w/ chips, drink popcorn, cupcakes candied nuts $13

MEALS/FOOD EXPENSES

Breakfast	Lunch	Dinner

MEALS/FOOD EXPENSES

Breakfast	Lunch	Dinner

MEALS/FOOD EXPENSES

Breakfast	Lunch	Dinner

MEALS/FOOD EXPENSES

Breakfast	Lunch	Dinner

MEALS/FOOD EXPENSES

Breakfast	Lunch	Dinner

MEALS/FOOD EXPENSES

Breakfast	Lunch	Dinner

NOTES

NOTES

NOTES

Made in the USA
Monee, IL
04 November 2026

67381375R00036